MEDITATION & DREAMS

(for fairly normal people)

by
Paul Desmond

Published by Sarum Publishers
8 Innes Road, Observatory, 2198. R.S.A.

ISBN 0-620-17076-X

First Edition 1992
First Impression 2000
Second Impression 4000

Printed by: Atlas Printers - 83 Pine Street, Durban 4001

INTRODUCTION

This book is designed to hopefully be easy on the eyes, easy on the mind and easy on the spirit.

I especially hope that it in some way gives you a feeling of space and a sense of peace.

Maybe a little inspiration even, just like any meditation should.

Paul '91

*.....to all the meditation teachers and students
I've been lucky enough to know over the years.....*

BEGINNINGS

*When I first heard about meditation, I was immediately suspicious.
I found myself visualising all sorts of odd-bods with rubber legs
waiting for me. So when I went to the meditation centre and was
greeted by a serene and beautiful young woman called Christine, I
was a little taken aback.*

*We sat down and she began to explain, "Meditation is just a
process of creating more loving thoughts." She looked at me and I
noticed just how peaceful her eyes were. She went on, "Whether it's
more loving thoughts about the self or others, or life in general,
meditation is the time we give to create these thoughts."*

*"The first step is to see everyone as a soul and to try to understand
the good in them. To see that each soul is just like you, another
being just trying to be peaceful and happy." She looked into my
eyes with her clear, steady gaze and I realised straightaway just
how much understanding this practice had given her.*

*Her eyes had a light of happiness in them that I'd never seen
before. She wasn't just talking, she was living it.*

It was so real.

*I found that the more I looked at people like this, the more it seemed
that everyone had something amazing to share with me. Whether
young or old, it was as if there was a magic in them. Until then I'd
always been rather cynical: if there had been a way of recognising
what a moron they were I definitely would have discovered it, but
suddenly I found myself appreciating the strangest people.*

Even old ladies and foreigners!

The Sister

I remember her eyes sparkling
As she said "Hello".
Looking at life,
The future, the past.
Her joy shone,
Her laugh was so light.
What does it mean
To know who we are?
How does it feel
To say "I am peace"?

Her eyes echoed my answer.

We are souls
We are brothers
We are peace.

Children

There's a child
That I saw
Dancing in the mists
Of a river.
Free and happy
Beyond all imagining.
And her presence
Was like a star
That held me entranced
With the softness of its light.

The Wise Man

The chimes at the skylight
Speaking to the wind
Echo the distance of the thoughts
That wander through his mind.

The almost fragile lines upon his face,
Reflect an inner radiance
As he climbs ever higher
Over fresh levels of experience.

Silhouetted against this world
He seems to shine brighter
As he quietly sits
So detached and sublime.

In this world
But not of it —
Eternal child
Of another more golden time.

TURNING POINTS
The Need for More

I often found myself wondering how I got stuck with meditation. I mean being a fairly normal person and all that. In fact, looking at my life, I came to see to a certain extent I'd been set up for it. First of all, I guess certain events happened to me that made me very suspicious about the general direction of everybody's consciousness.

I think the first was when I was twelve years old. This fat, ugly girl from around the corner fell in love with me. She would ring me up every evening, saying, "I love you, I love you, I can't live without you. I'm going to die..." And she whined and cried on the phone every night for two months. I remember my big sister telling me that that's what life's all about.

When I was thirteen, I remember the police coming home on a disturbance of the peace call to break up one of my family's "little altercations" as my mother used to call them. I could feel "happily ever after" wasn't all it was made out to be.

When I was fourteen, I started wondering who'd talked me into thinking I was James Dean and wanting to die young.

Things began to change when I was fifteen that's when I went to my first rock concert. There was a beautiful light show with the most incredible music and there was an atmosphere of, how can I say, thousands of people coming together in one deep feeling.

I think from that point the only thing I wanted was pure experience, and I slowly realised that we need something more. More than all these amazing facts they are teaching us in school; more than this whole society based on strange and unusual attainments; that deep down we need more, we need pure experience.

The turning point was seeing that it's our state of mind that matters and that's something more.

Echoes In The Wind

And did you ever
Sit in the silence
And hold on to the moment
To the experience
That filled your mind
With a joy
You could never explain.....

Something Is Missing

What then the toys of men?
Something is missing.
We've classified and categorised
Labels and fables.

We move faster than the lions,
Cut through the skies above,
Dive so deeply in the ocean,
We've forgotten how to love.

What then the lives of men?
The love link is missing,
The bridges have been broken down
And no one is crossing.

Sure we've crawled across our history,
Scrambling orphans in the dust
Tired and trembling and broken down.
We've forgotten how to trust.

TURNING POINTS
Eternity

The next big turning point was at Paddington Street Underground. Now, I suppose Paddington Station is a turning point for a lot of people. For me, it was a little different.

I was sitting on the platform reading a book about life after death written by Colin Wilson. In it Colin had datarised research by a number of scientists who had all studied strange and unusual phenomena and had ended up believing in life after death.

As I finished this book, the evidence for life after death was so deep and clear I found that I couldn't chuck it all in the bin. It dawned on me as I was walking across the station to my train that maybe I'm not just Paul Desmond blundering around Paddington Station but I might be eternal. I just couldn't get rid of this idea.

There I was on the last train to Wembley convinced I was eternal!

Words

You can say valley,
But does it bring the experience
Of the groves of the trembling golden aspen
Nestling like children in the valley slopes?

Does it show you crystal clear rivers
That taste of youth
Leaping and moving
Fresh against the timeless mossy rocks?

Does it show you the endless sweep of mountains
Huge and age carven,
The bright white sunlight
Suffusing the yellow gold land,
The heat haze of pollen
Hanging weary in the air?

And there's a cloud shadow
Miles away moving,
Ethereal over the trees.

"Souls don't die"
If that's all I could say,
I'd say it.

The cloud moves over me
With its fleeting texture
And then it's gone,
And then it's gone.

We never die.
We never die.

We never die...

REALISATIONS

Another turning point for me came when I was sixteen; I'd just left the house of a friend who'd attempted suicide and I was thinking how so few people are really happy or even able to succeed in their relationships. It was at that time that it really hit me that the only thing we are experiencing is our thoughts and life is heaven or hell because of them. I just felt that we needed training in learning how to love ourselves and where we are and what we do. If we can't somehow surround ourselves with beautiful thoughts, how will we ever find beautiful places and people?

As I walked home through this vast high-rise housing estate, the place was so violent and so lonely in the rain and yet I felt so good.

*If we can't surround ourselves with beautiful thoughts,
how will we ever find beautiful places and people?*

More - Our Ideals and Dreams

It's a love
beyond words.

It's a peace
that stills your soul.

It's a happiness
that shares and warms.

It's a purity
clear and wholesome.

It's a truth
that will always love and understand.

It's a feeling so good
so good
it echoes
over and over

Even in my dreams.

GROWING

The next time I sat with Christine, she started talking about how we need an aim for the self. I'd always thought that you learned how to drink and smoke with the lads and you were adult and that was that. But Christine started speaking about things like developing regard and patience. She also mentioned inner strength and the ability to control one's thoughts and feelings. When she got around to the subject of remaining cheerful it dawned on me just how much we can grow, that if we just have an inner goal, we can change.

In fact, ultimately we can be whoever we want to be.

The Temple

The temple is full of bliss,
The temple is full of peace.
Its walls are love,
Its foundation purity.
Its decoration are the tapestries
Of understanding and knowledge.
Its windows are the outlook
That sees only the virtuous and sublime.
Its incense is the fragrance
That fills you with dreams of love to build.
Its lights are flames
That are patient and enduring.
Its doors are firm and true
And open to all with love and respect.
Its stairs are humble
And serve all.
And lastly the temple
Is set high on a hill serene and detached.

The temple so high and fair,
The temple is you.

Do you remember who you are?

WHAT IS LOVE ANYWAY?

Lesson 3 with Christine was about methods of loving other people. I'd always thought love was a fairly basic thing. I'd had this mental image of someone who was mind-stunningly attractive and very wise and especially appreciative of five foot five men with acne like me. I thought that this would be the right recipe for love. However, I'd unfortunately never come across this type of love. When Christine heard about this she quietly pointed out that all I was doing was shopping for all the things I hadn't got; this was unfortunately very true.

She said, "Love is a giving, and making yourself the gift that can be given. Whether to a person or place, or even an era."

I think in some ways we have to redefine the totality of love and maybe we should all go crazy and try and teach it in schools.

Sun Shafts

Love is understanding
Love is understanding what moves people
Love is understanding why it moves them
Love is understanding enough
To be one of the things that moves them too.

You and Me

Life,
It's such an incredible long time.
I must have been a hundred people,
In the last ten years.
With you.

And you know me?

The music plays,
I feel so much,
Life unfolds,
And I can't explain.
I see your eyes,
And our history echoes.
Did we share so much,
Where the time goes?

And I know you,
And you know me.

Two Become One

The light in the sky
At the year's waning
The happiness in your eyes
Calling to me
The sun sparkling
On the rivers flow
Reminding me of all the memories
That you taught me to know.

And
How sweet is your love
And
How deep is your peace.

And the haunting shades of pink
That edge the November twilight
Remind me how very close
And known I feel to you.
As I wander with you
Under the giant red oaks
And the shafts of sunlight
Dappling their stretching avenue

Are beautiful, like the life before us.

LOVE OF LIFE
The Meaning of Life and Other Confusions

*The next time I went to the centre I came across this older lady
called Anthea and she was talking about love of life. Now it's not
necessarily that easy, is it? I was thinking about my father
especially. He wakes up every morning and there's the wife snoring
and he rolls over and the next thing he sees is her false teeth in a
jar. He staggers downstairs and drops himself in the daily rag
newspaper and then he blunders off into the rush hour... I mean,
where does one love life in that situation?*

*As Anthea talked about love and life she pointed out that the world
is the most incredibly beautiful place and it's exactly what we make
it. In the same way, with all the people, it's how much we want to
enjoy them.*

*Then she led me outside with a laugh and showed me this old bloke
whose job was to wave the children across the road. It was
amazing that he was so happy with his little lot - he'd greet every
car that went past and the car drivers would toot back because
they knew him. He'd also wave the kids up and down and across
the road and they'd all greet him and laugh. He was really enjoying
it. I watched him there with the most mindlessly stupid job I could
think of but it was as Anthea had said, it's exactly what you make
it; it's all about your attitude. You can count it good, or you can
count it bad, it's up to you.*

*Up until then, I'd been convinced that happiness cost an absolute
fortune and had never imagined that even nerds at zebra crossings
could love life!*

Everything changes with love

Everything.

The Observer - Love of Life

The haze on the distant tracks
The quiet of the Sun
And a lone figure
Sitting in the shadows
Filled with peace.

The autumn leaves blowing golden
From the swaying banks of trees
Like the thoughts
Falling from my mind
Touched by yet another breeze.

Swirling down,
Swirling down...

The light on the distant hillside
Awakens all kinds of memories
Like the detachment I feel
Surrounded by all their angry madness
Surrounded by the things they say are sorrow
I just didn't feel a flicker in my love.

And quietly with eyes
That have to be open
Like the mind
That just has to wonder
I watch the rivers and the mountains
And all the works of man.

Swirling and drifting
Timelessly down...

With a love
That words can't describe.

The Mountain

I was thinking of the sunset
The banks of gold stretching endless
Behind the deepening silhouettes.

I was thinking of all the souls
Who'd gazed with such love
Onto those glowing scenes.

And sitting in the cool twilight
Feeling so grateful
Just to know you
Just to know you.

And I was thinking how close
I felt to you
With all the visions in me
I can't explain.

And gazing on a flying bird
Soaring freely in the sky
Seeming so effortless in its flight.

I was remembering the shadows
That seem to dance in your eyes
Mirroring the love that was within.

And I was feeling like a river
That seemed to run beyond time
With its murmuring voice to your ocean.

And I was gazing on my future
Filled so full by my past
Just waiting, just waiting for more.

This thing of appreciation is a big thing.

Feel

The night is late,
My friends have come and gone.
The lights are dim,
And the evening shadows long.
And I'm so peaceful,
With my life before me.
And my guitar sounds
Soft and light.
And I murmur the words
To the long still night

Make it pure,
Make it good.
Make it pure,
Make it good.

And a silent gentle breeze
Touches my hair
Like a mother.

The world is the most incredibly beautiful place and it's exactly what we make it. In the same way, with all the people, it's how much we want to enjoy them.

POSITIVE THINKING

The next time that I saw Christine. she explained what powerful meditation is. I was particularly worried as to whether I was going to have to breathe through my earholes, or tie my legs in a reef knot or something.

Christine explained that powerful meditation is just to sit with clear. determined thoughts that mean a lot to you, and to work with those thoughts until they create feelings - for instance. thinking over and over about peace or contentment until they flow into your feelings. actions and life.

"In the same way." she said "a lot of people meditate negatively. thinking over and over things like 'I'm all alone.' or 'no one loves me.' or 'I've been through so much,' and these thoughts take over their whole lives."

I remember Christine looking at me and saying with real force that. if you create a powerful thought every day with deep reverence. it becomes a power that dwarfs all your problems and carries you higher than you can dream of.

It's a bit like lying on your back and staring at the stars - and the longer you're there. the more there's only the stars. that space. that peace and a beauty that humbles you.

Meditation

Silence dawns
Vibrant with experience.
We sit humbled
By our depths of feeling
Gazing into
The skies of our thoughts
And time and space softly fade

Into being.

Meditation

*It's like lying on your back and staring at the stars and
the longer you're there the more there's only the stars,
that space, that peace and a beauty that humbles you.....*

WHAT ABOUT GOD?

When Christine started talking about God, I must admit my only memory of Him was being told at a young age, by my grandfather, that if I ever believed in Him, I'd get a good thrashing. I'd always had a funny idea about God being sort of like an old bloke with thunderbolts for eyebrows and eyes like security cameras.

The first thing that made me re-evaluate my idea of God after learning to meditate was my counselling work. I used to counsel drug addicts because all my friends were drug addicts and also suicidals because all my friends were suicidal as well. Slowly I came to notice that only the ones who said from the heart "God help me," would get power. I watched this happen a number of times and I began to wonder.

The second thing I noticed was that I was getting regularly collared by religious nutters - singing ones, clapping ones, ones with books, ones without hair and on and on. I sometimes thought that God sent them all to me to practise how to irritate strangers. Anyway, after months of this, I started thinking that since time began, people have been talking about God... Why?

The third thing that worried me was seeing how people always turned to God when there was absolutely nowhere else to go. Even if they didn't believe in God it was as if there was something in them that was more intelligent and knew where to go when there was a big problem.

Now I think that it's a very personal thing for each one to determine what exactly God is, and that that's entirely up to each one of us to work out for ourselves. Yet, I found that even when I wanted to get away from God he kept popping up.

Christine said, "The whole thing about meditation is to learn to love God again — whether you're Christian or Moslem or whatever, to within that, love your God and think about his glory."

Enter
(Engraved on the doors of some old Churches)

Enter this door
As if the floor
Within were gold,
And every wall
Of jewels all
Of wealth untold
As if a choir
In robes of fire
Were singing here
Nor shout, nor rush,
But hush.....
For God is here.

The Heart of Islam

And faraway the Muslim cries
And his love of Allah
Resounds to the sky.
And the sunrise
Over the lonely desert's dunes
Shimmers on the diamond studded mosque
Making it something more than human.

And who knows what they feel there?
And who knows of their love?

And the sand eddies alone in the desert
And his eyes were like jewels
You could see his heart
Burning in them.
And closer and closer
The men of flowing robes
Move on Haj to Mecca.

And who knows what they feel there?
And who knows of their love?

And what of that gateway
To another shining world
That stands alone amid the sand,
Haunting the lives of a hundred nations?

Touching Forever
(An Eternal Love)

The blades of summer grass
Yellow in the sun.
Sway, just audible
Softly in the heat.

The ripples on the lake
Murmur on the bank
And the swans glide
Their images wash my mind.

And there's the sense
Of eternity
Stretching away.

And this love has ever been
Before they first cried out to God
Before they raised the pyramids
Before the land of the moon
Before the lords of the sun.

This love has ever been.....

LOVE OF GOD

*I remember, as Christine talked about God, her eyes misted over
and she seemed to gaze into the distance. I could feel a profound
love and purity radiating from her. She started speaking. "The
easiest way to meditate on God is to picture Him as a light of love, a
place that knows the beginning, the middle, the end of me and
understands." She smiled and went on. "It's also good to see God
as an unlimited peace, a stillness so calming and healing for your
mind. Also to see God as purity, something so high and good. All
your sorrows are left behind in front of such a clear
wholesomeness."*

*Looking at Christine, her face sparkling with her experience of God.
I could feel I loved her God and it made sense, if not to my head
then definitely to my heart.*

The whole thing about meditation is to learn to love God again, that's all.

Images

If His love were a place,
It would be lost
In the thunder of the waves at sunrise.

If His bliss could take form,
it would be like an eagle soaring
Higher and higher over the cool mountain peaks.

If His knowledge should touch you,
It would be like thousands of doors opening
Onto the horizons of wonder.

And if His stillness should hold you,
You'll know by the incredible freshness
And clarity that floods your mind.

The easiest way to meditate on God is to picture Him as a light of love, a place that knows the beginning, the middle, the end of me and understands.

DESTINY

The last time I saw Christine was in the garden and I remember her talking about destiny as the shadows from the trees spread over the grass. She said, "One of the best things we can be lucky enough to have in our lives is something to truly live for, even something to die for; and the greatest emptiness today, is many people don't even have something to look forward to. And we, knowing God, have to understand that we come from that perfection and are destined to go back there."

Sunshafts

First there was perfect stillness
And in that stillness
Shone the light and might
Of five things.

Peace.
Bliss.
Purity.
Love.
Understanding.

And as you wander alone
Through the dramas of space and time,
People, people,
Know you not your home?

Destiny

And the seekers seek
And the lovers love
As if they had
Any choice.
Like the tree
That reaches for the sun
Or the stars
That burn so bright.
We know what
We are to be
We know what
We are to be.

And there's just a figure
Alone.
And the path of his heart
Before him.
Reaching through the mists
Of another world.
Into a light
That merges every outline.

The final destiny of love
Is inescapable.

One of the best things we can be lucky enough to have in our lives is something to truly live for, even something to die for.

Fortune

By the silence of His presence
By the stillness of Its peace.
I was thinking
Of all the souls who've come.
And merged within this love
Shine ever brighter in its light.

And we're like the swans
That fly south
To the stretching gold clouds,
Until time itself is changed.

And His light fills my eyes,
After so long in the night.
And the skies of His Mind
And the echo of His Love
Is woven on my soul
For all eternity.

And standing
At the very end of time
Gazing at this
Unlimited world before me
I know such joy
At my future destiny.

CHANGES

As time passed by I found myself enjoying meditation a great deal, although how I ended up teaching it is a complete mystery to me. But I often remember the last words Christine said as I left for South Africa to teach meditation. "The moment you live something you're teaching it whether you want to or not."

FAITH

I think one of the worst things that happens to a lot of us is that, as the years go by, we get caught in situations where we stop feeling happy or fulfilled and we just get used to that. It's as if we give up even on ourselves.

It's true that you can achieve anything you like if you believe you can. I remember opening a meditation centre in Soweto in South Africa just because everyone said that it was impossible. People were saying that they'd kill me or set fire to me. Now, I've always liked people who are direct, anyway! So you've just got to believe in yourself, you've just got to believe that it can all change and never give up trying.

Soweto '88

Believe In Yourself

The endless view over the clouds,
From the snow on the mountain peak.
The rush as they tell you
You're in a field of your own.

The palms of old Sri Lanka
Where the sunset waves
Are just another vision
Where the people care,
With the ease of simplicity.

And they said you'd never know them all,
And they said you'd never know them all.

The dandelion seed that drifts sunlit
Across my field of vision
Bringing back the love
Of the one I shared an eternity with.

The meditation in the stillness
Of another timeless world
Where you have no form
And move forever into peace.

And they said we couldn't get there,
And they said we couldn't get there.

The distant trees
Merging their different shades.
Two falcons
Flying free to the sky.

And they said it would rain today,
You know I just don't believe them anymore.

The Politics of Ecstacy

The row of windows
Shining with muted light.
Shaft their gentle rays
On the eyes of my vision
And I feel a cool gaze
Fall over mine.
And someone else I love
Murmurs "Everything shows in a face"

And I must have listened for hours
As they said you couldn't teach love,
As they said you couldn't teach purity.
As they argued endless
That people don't change.

And all the while my mind
Drifted through the golden memories.
Of the shining house of light
Where so many souls.
Were made over anew
Filled by the silence
Of their peace and bliss.

And I knew it wasn't so,
And I knew it wasn't so.

Believe in yourself.

TOUCHING

I think for me another interesting aspect of teaching people to meditate was reaching people. I don't just mean being with them and talking. But being egoless enough to really hear their sorrows and happinesses. to be silent enough to just understand and be there. To be able to touch them and let them know that they are not alone even with their feelings.

Durban '86

Reaching Others

There's a picture
In the sunrises of my mind
Of a perfect state
Of clear cool being
And it's hanging,
Hanging crooked in my mind.

And there's this angel,
This beautiful being
I've never known,
And she's so light
Moving ethereally —
Always just a fleeting glimpse.

And there's the sense
Of emptiness
Where there was
A presence

And there's the sense
Of emptiness
Where there was
A presence.

And the picture,
The picture hangs straight.

The Rebirth of a Soul

The distant thunder sounds
Rolling ominous over the desert
There's a stillness in the air
You can almost touch
Everything is waiting
Everything is waiting.

And as the sheets of rain
Begin to fall
The land is silent
And still and receiving.

And far away I remember
The day the thought finally dawns
That after all
My life's in my hands
And I know where it's going
And nothing and no one can stop me.

And as the sheets of rain
Continue to fall
I seem to see through them
As if they were a window
A window in my mind.

And later
Maybe a day
Or maybe a lifetime

After the rain has gone
The red gold sunlight shines on
Like flames on the skyline

Deserts can bloom. even human ones.

HEALING

Being a teacher of meditation, I often find myself associating with the not-so-mentally stable. I suppose people imagine I'm the right person to see when they're feeling a bit crazy!

Anyway, one night a colleague rang and asked me to come over quickly. On arriving I found a very dear friend, called Lisa, whom I hadn't seen for a while. She was wrapped in a blanket, gazing into space, her face streaked with tears. I spoke but she didn't seem to hear. Eventually I spent about three weeks with her, in which time I had to pull her off balconies, save her from motorcars even once extinguish the flames she'd set on herself. Slowly the psychiatrists got her more and more doped out until finally the day came when they said we should commit her.

I remember as Lisa and I walked into the Mental Hospital, she sort of sensed what was going on and I could just feel terror from her. She gripped my hand and it was strange but I started feeling the same way. It was just so incredibly cold — patients doped senseless and nurses marching around. Lisa looked at me and for the first time in weeks said, with the voice and the manner I'd always known and loved her for, "Just give me a chance, please just give me a chance."

I had to think very hard about whether what I was doing was right or wrong — if I had any right to ignore all those doctors with all their machines. She just sat there looking so sane with her soul in her eyes, pleading. Finally, I snapped: I grabbed her and her bag and just ran. We left her pills and everything else behind and went with her best friend to a farm.

Ultimately she came through; it seemed that love and a break were the answer. I still don't know if what I did was right and I certainly wouldn't advise others to do the same. But I remember Lisa saying to me, months later, "Paul, it all taught me just how much we need to look after ourselves, and even more than that how much we need to listen to ourselves."

Since then I've realised that two things are very precious: friends who value your happiness more than theirs and the necessity to look after oursleves, never sacrificing our happiness for any reason.

Cape Town '89

Be good to yourself, you're all you've got

The Language of the Soul

She put her hand
To my cheek
Raised her eyes to meet mine
And called to my soul

Just give me a chance

Just give me a chance.

Listening

And how often
Do you really speak?
And how often
Do you really hear?
And how often
Do you really touch?
And how often
Do you really move yourself

And others?

DREAMS

*After I'd been in South Africa a couple of years I brought a
multi-racial delegation to the mountain headquarters where we
teach. Sitting on this mountain all of us were no longer racial
groups, we were just one family with one feeling of peace. We were
sitting there with a deep feeling of unity. We could share more in
one glance than I could have done in a lifetime before I learnt to
meditate.*

Himalaya Foothills '87

The Highest Place

The heat of the desert sun
The endless joy as you know you've arrived
The sound of the inner stillness
Merging to the stretching horizons.

How can we have reached so high?

The still of the early morning
The sense of meeting and knowing
The waves of vibrations raining down
So much more love than I can accept.

How can we hold so much?

The mists of the northern mountains
The union I know with your peace
The cool of the fragrant halls
Where the soul goes so much further.

How can we have gone so far?

The taste of the dawn chill on the air
The life of an infinite vision
The warmth of the sunlit shafts
Falling on this land of revelation.

Thank you.
Thank you.

JOURNEYS

I like this space where two people experience just one feeling or where one person gets merged in the experience of his or her surroundings. I remember being at the release from a reformatory school of one young meditation student who'd been studying at our university for two years. This child and I had journeyed from her being a knife-wielding thug who'd never known kindness through all the discoveries that had led to her being a caring women and successful student. And, standing at the gate, we shared the most incredible feeling of happiness. We could have stood there forever.

Newcastle '88

Leaving

A lone cedar
Outlined on the horizon,
A plume of stratus cloud
Against the blue of the summer skies,
The 9.00 a.m. sunlignt
Bouncing off the endless empty road.
There's so much we know
And never talk of,
There's so much we know
Without realising.

The fresh breeze
Occasionally spiralling
Our thoughts far away.
Drifting
Amid the golden memories
Of all we've seen
Amid the sheer happiness
Of knowing dreams
Can be.

And our eyes meet
And how they share
And we are going
Like innocent strangers
To a world
That can know sorrow.
And our voices crackle
With soft richness
Tying us together
Amidst the endless stretching
Horizons.
And just how much
Have we both come to know?

And it's strange
The way only such a very few
Know this incredible
Beauty.

It's so strange.

LETTING GO

Once I was teaching at a dancing school. I started off my lecture talking about how I really admire their pleux aixs and faux pas and the whole place absolutely broke up with laughter. Eventually someone pointed out that a faux pas is not a ballet movement — well, how was I supposed to know that sort of thing? They were laughing a lot and the whole lecture went on like that: people were literally rolling up in tears. After all the happiness, there was one woman left behind in the corner, crying. I asked her why she was crying and she said, "Because I'm happy." Logical, I thought so I asked, "You're crying tears of sorrow because you're happy?" She agreed and left.

Afterwards I thought about it some more and I felt that so many of us are unhappy on such a deep level that it's as if our minds are not our friends anymore. We think thoughts that hurt us and drag around terrible things from the past. I find that meditation with its positivity gives us a mirror where we can see how we make ourselves unhappy, and start cutting it out.

I think letting go of sorrow is one of the most beautiful things I've ever seen happen to people - when they let go of guilt and blame and because of that let go of the past.

Table Mountain '90

Everything Changes

As I wandered through the forests
I saw a woodland fawn
Frozen to stillness by my approach
His heart beating
His breath steaming
Amid the sunlit dews of morning.

And faraway in my heart
The blades of grass
Were growing over the ruins
Of sorrow's many halls.

And there was but a movement
In the air
And a sound in the trees
And the fawn,
The beautiful fawn was gone.

And far away the blades of grass
Have grown.
And this old heart feels new once more.

TOMORROWS

Meditation is a journey inside to the horizons of the spirit.
Horizons of a better you, of more beautiful relationships, of a sense of love for God.
I remember someone once said "Prayer is when you talk to God and meditation is when you listen".

That's it — we aren't trying to achieve the incredible but rather to go on a quiet journey where we can love some of these inner horizons within ourselves and others.

Arise

And I look
On life:
Its myriad acts,
Its myriad scenes.
And there's a shining
In my eye
At the sweetness
Of your soul.

And there's so much more
Than they know here.
So much life
In forgotten loves.
And I watch
Two hands touch.
And I watch
Two doves soar.

And I watch a man
Turn to light
And still with wonder
Fill with bliss,
Fill with bliss.

Filled with bliss.

And deep down
There's a wave of peace
That grows
And grows
To fill the cathedral
Of my soul.

Meditation is a journey inside to the horizons of the spirit.

Good Luck

Biodata

Paul Desmond has been a meditation student with the Brahma Kumaris World Spiritual University for the last twelve years. Many of the experiences within the book are drawn from his practise of meditation, both in England and South Africa.

The University is a non-sectarian, non-political body active in some 65 countries. It regularly runs courses in subjects such as:

- Self Development
- The Art of Meditation
- The Power of Relationships
- The Awareness of Destiny

These courses are to a high degree the basis of many of the experiences within the book. However, not all the statements within the book need necessarily be those of the University. More information can be gained at any of the University branches below.

Johannesburg	(011) 854-4904	8 Innes Road, Observatory, 2198
Durban	(031) 84-5150	3 Bailey Road, Redhill, 4051
Cape Town	(021) 47-8787	22 Kylemore Road, Woodstock, 7925
Port Elizabeth	(041) 47-1322	178 Mountainrise Ave, Malabar, 6020